ADVANCING THE RULE OF LAW ⬦ A CENTURY OF EXCELLENCE AT

EMORY LAW

ADVANCING THE RULE OF LAW: A CENTURY OF EXCELLENCE AT EMORY LAW

EMORY UNIVERSITY SCHOOL OF LAW

1301 Clifton Road, Atlanta, Georgia 30322
www.law.emory.edu

Robert A. Schapiro
Dean & Asa Griggs Candler Professor of Law

Robert Ahdieh
Vice Dean & K. H. Gyr Professor
of Private International Law

EMORY LAW PUBLICATION TEAM

Susan Clark
Associate Dean for Marketing and Communications

Contributors
Alyssa Ashdown
Mark Engsberg
Martha Fagan
A. Kenyatta Greer
Gary Hauk
Vanessa King

BOOK DEVELOPMENT TEAM

Michele C. Marill
Author

Rob Levin
Editor

Renée Peyton
Archivist and Production

Bob Land
Copyediting

Shoshana Hurwitz
Indexing

Rick Korab
Book and Jacket Design

BOOKHOUSE
GROUP, INC.

Bookhouse Group, Inc.
www.bookhouse.net

Printed in the USA using soy-based ink on acid-free, high archival paper carrying chain-of-custody certification from the Forest Stewardship Council (FSC), Sustainable Forestry Initiative (SFI), and the Programme for the Endorsement of Forest Conservation (PEFC).

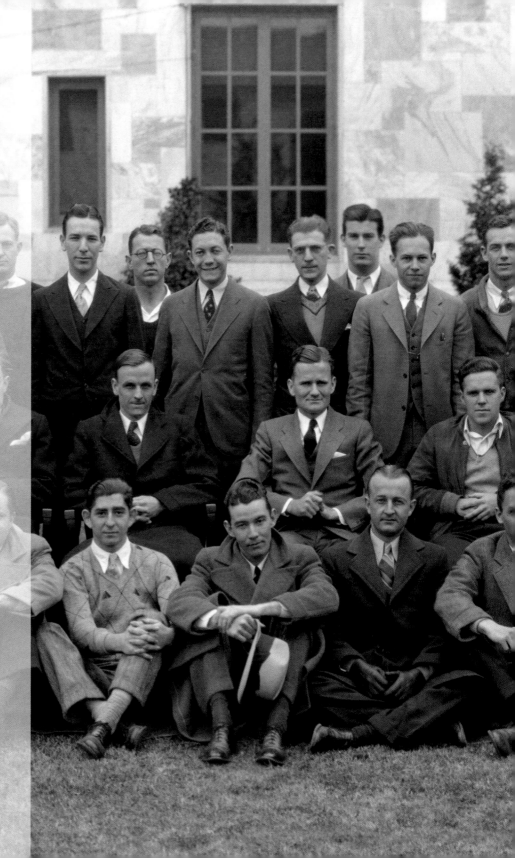

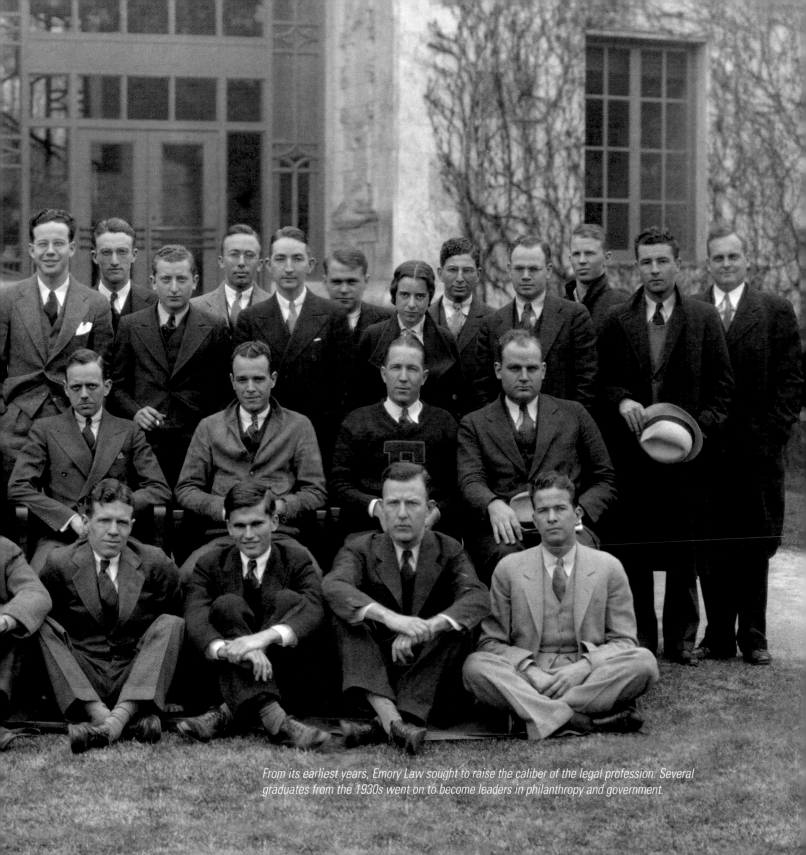

From its earliest years, Emory Law sought to raise the caliber of the legal profession. Several graduates from the 1930s went on to become leaders in philanthropy and government.

CONTENTS

Class of 2016 graduates Evyn Rabinowitz, Jewel Quintyne, and Ryan Pulley at Emory Law Diploma Ceremony, held May 9, 2016.

Emory Law students gain valuable practice posing arguments in moot court and mock trial. The competitions began in the classroom, but today, moot court and mock trial teams compete across the country. Emory Law hosts an annual Civil Rights and Liberties Moot Court Competition.

FOREWORD

One hundred years ago, a group of educators and lawyers had a vision to elevate the standards of the legal profession. In the words of then–Emory University chancellor Bishop Warren A. Candler, they aimed to inspire lawyers to carry forth more boldly "the ethics and ideals of an ancient and honorable profession."

Today, as Emory Law celebrates its centennial, I am proud of the remarkable ways in which we have fulfilled that charge. From its earliest days, Emory Law graduates became leaders in government and philanthropy. Eléonore Raoul 20L campaigned for women's suffrage and later helped found the Atlanta League of Women Voters. Randolph Thrower 36L, a prominent tax attorney, became commissioner of the Internal Revenue Service—and resigned rather than allow President Richard Nixon to use the IRS to punish his political enemies.

After Emory Law dean Ben Johnson 40L, with Henry L. Bowden 34L, argued the landmark case that desegregated Georgia's private colleges and universities, Johnson focused on making Emory Law a leader in race and gender diversity. Ted Smith 65L, the first black student at Emory Law, enrolled in the law school in the fall of 1963. Soon after, Johnson convinced Marvin Arrington 67L and Clarence Cooper 67L to transfer from Howard University School of Law in Washington, DC, to Emory Law. Arrington later became president of the Atlanta City Council and a Fulton County Superior Court judge. Cooper is a senior United States district judge.

Emory Law still embodies that spirit of bold action as it strives to prepare lawyers to be leading members of the Bar. The Kessler-Eidson Program for Trial Techniques pioneered an intense hands-on experience of trial advocacy, and Emory Law was the first law school in the country to introduce a comprehensive transactional skills curriculum. Six legal clinics engage students to use their skills for the public good, and students perform many hours of pro bono work on behalf of indigent and underrepresented groups.

What its founders may not have envisioned were the myriad ways in which Emory Law would shape and define legal scholarship and thought. Consider just two examples: the Center for the Study of Law and Religion introduced a new field of study in 1982, advancing our understanding of the role of religion in shaping law, politics, and society. A further milestone came in 2004, when the Feminism and Legal Theory Project moved to Emory Law, and more recently with the foundation of the Vulnerability & the Human Condition Initiative, which has established vulnerability as a critical framework for understanding the human condition. Elsewhere, from constitutional law, civil procedure, and torts to election law, health law, and technological innovation and patent law, Emory Law professors have published the leading academic texts.

As we celebrate this important anniversary, we seek to honor the many contributions of our talented faculty, staff, students, and alumni. Truly, they have elevated the legal profession—not just in the United States, but across the world.

The political polarization, global strife, and rapid technological change that mark our current era underscore the critical mission set forth a century ago. Advancing the rule of law has never been more important. As we look forward to our next century, Emory Law will continue to prepare generations of lawyers who are dedicated to forging a better society and to upholding the highest standards of our honorable profession.

Robert A. Schapiro

Robert A. Schapiro
Dean & Asa Griggs Candler Professor of Law

The Judge Elbert Tuttle Courtroom in Gambrell Hall provides a lifelike setting for the Kessler-Eidson Program for Trial Techniques, an award-winning program that teaches trial advocacy.

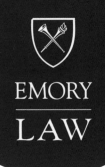

CHAPTER ONE

Advancing the Rule of Law

The prospective jurors slouched in two rows of chairs, staring intently, twelve pairs of eyes fixed on the young lawyer at the podium. Holland Stewart 17L took a casual and friendly stance. He tried hard not to let his inexperience show.

In a David-versus-Goliath case, a suit over trademark infringement, he needed to select jurors who were sympathetic to the little guys of the world. He zeroed in on one who ran a small recording studio. "Have you ever had problems with large businesses encroaching on your business?" he asked.

"They always have more budget for advertisement, and they grab my customers," the man said sullenly.

Learning often extends beyond the classroom, leveraging the expertise of dedicated alumni and other expert practitioners.

"I'm sorry to hear about that," Stewart said, not altogether sorry, but trying to figure out how this would fit into his strategy. A good prospect—or perhaps too good? Did he just give the defense a reason to cut the man from the jury pool? Did he ask enough questions? Too many?

The moment felt authentic—played out before a "judge" looking down from the massive wooden bench. Realism was precisely the point of this coaching session for second-year students at Emory University School of Law.

Practicing law is an art—and also a carefully crafted problem of logic, a science of evidence, a study of the human mind, a deep dive into legal theory or case history. Since its founding in 1916, Emory University School of Law has engaged its students with these complexities

Practicing law is an art—and also a carefully crafted problem of logic, a science of evidence, a study of the human mind, a deep dive into legal theory or case history. Since its founding in 1916, Emory University School of Law has engaged its students with these complexities while giving young lawyers the practical skills they need to succeed.

while giving them the practical skills they need to succeed.

Yet Emory Law also pushes the boundaries—by defining new legal spheres, embracing diversity, and encouraging innovation in legal thought and education. The Kessler-Eidson Program for Trial Techniques—the litigation skills class that is required for all second-year students, known as 2Ls—was groundbreaking when it began in 1982 and remains a national and even international model, regularly hosting visitors from Russia, Korea, China, Mexico,

continued on page 6

Learning to Think Like a Lawyer
A Legacy of Excellence in Teaching

At eleven o'clock, Sanford Bishop 71L took his seat in Professor Bill Ferguson's Civil Procedure class. It was the late 1960s, and the air was already thick with trepidation. Ferguson, with his gray mutton-chop sideburns and gruff drawl, taught his class in the classic Socratic method, posing layers of questions to tremulous 1Ls. Bishop studied hard to prepare for Ferguson's class.

Sanford Bishop 71L

> # "You should always stick to your guns. If you think you're right, don't give up!"
>
> ## —*Professor Bill Ferguson*

On this day, Ferguson presented a hypothetical case and asked the ultimate question: Who wins, and why? A student gave an answer. "That's ridiculous," he said dismissively. Student after student failed to satisfy Ferguson. Finally, he called on Bishop.

"When I gave my answer, he started to yell and he banged on the desk and he said, 'That is asinine, Mr. Bishop! How could you say something with such cockfoolery?'

"I shot back at him, as sharp as he had shot at me. We went at it for about two or three minutes, back and forth. I could feel all the students who were sitting around me lean away from me. I decided I should back off the limb I had gone out on. I gradually backtracked on my position.

Professor Bill Ferguson

"Mr. Ferguson stopped. He picked up a piece of chalk, drew a circle on the chalkboard, and put an X in the circle. And he threw the chalk at the board and spun around.

"'That's too bad, Mr. Bishop, because you were right!' he shouted. 'Mr. Bishop, you should always stick to your guns. If you think you're right, don't give up!'"

Bishop never forgot that lesson—one that has served him well in his years as a civil rights lawyer and as a US congressman representing Southwest Georgia. He kept his cool when an Alabama judge pounded the bench and screamed at him. He stayed the course as he worked to improve prison conditions. And he stayed in touch with Ferguson, who taught at Emory Law from 1963 to 1998.

Ferguson was just one of a cadre of professors with a larger-than-life persona, faculty who devoted themselves to teaching law in their own distinct styles.

William "Doc" Agnor 37L was a portly Virginian with a resonant drawl and an ever-present cigar that he would rest on the edge of his desk or on the chalkboard as he taught. His students nicknamed him "Bull," for Agnor was a strong force during a teaching career that spanned from 1946 to 1981.

Agnor was especially supportive of women, who then

Professor William "Doc" Agnor 37L

made up a small minority of the enrollment. He had an encyclopedic memory, and Lucy McGough 66L recalls spending hours poring over case law to prepare when she became the first female faculty member at Emory Law in 1971. She was named a Charles Howard Candler Professor of Law in 1980.

Professor Don Fyr

"Nobody taught you how to teach law. You absorbed it by osmosis," says McGough, who taught at Emory for ten years, then became a professor at Louisiana State University, and later dean of Appalachian School of Law in Grundy, Virginia.

With long white hair, Don Fyr resembled a British barrister. He used a gentler version of the Socratic method to weave his lesson into an elaborate storytelling. "He had a talent for challenging and pushing students to their intellectual limit—without ever pushing so hard as to intimidate or embarrass," Andrew Klein 88L, now dean of Indiana University Robert H. McKinney School of Law, said in a memoriam after Fyr died in 1994.

The commonality between these longtime faculty members and others who followed in their path, if not their style, was a devotion to the art of teaching. "This faculty does an extraordinary job of teaching and mentoring," says Richard Freer, Robert Howell Hall Professor of Law, who counts Fyr as an inspiration.

Freer's own shelves are lined with a number of Emory Law "outstanding professor" awards, the Emory Scholar/ Teacher Award, and the university's highest teaching award: the Emory Williams Award for Excellence in Teaching. He is just one of many on the Emory Law faculty who continue the legacy of a deep commitment to educating the next generation of lawyers and leaders.

Classroom simulation has always been an important part of the Emory Law curriculum, but the opportunities to gain hands-on experience have multiplied.

continued from page 3

and other countries. In fact, Stewart's "jurors" were students from Shanghai Jiao Tong University who were learning about the US legal system. The professors were practicing attorneys who shared their real-life experiences.

Throughout its history, Emory Law has forged new ground, linking the law with disciplines such as economics, politics, and history, as well as advancing novel fields of study such as law and religion, feminism and legal theory, and vulnerability studies. In recent years, the curriculum has expanded dramatically, enabling greater specialization as well as new opportunities for experiential learning.

Students practice the art of negotiating and deal-making as they pursue the Transactional Law and Skills Certificate through the Center for Transactional Law and Practice. They gain hands-on experience in intellectual property law by joining teams of business students, engineers, and other innovators through Technological Innovation: Generating Economic Results (TI:GER), a joint program with the Georgia Institute of Technology. Students learn to view law in a broader social context, and in the Center for Federalism and Intersystemic Governance, they examine the interplay between multiple, overlapping levels of government.

At its centennial, Emory Law has much to celebrate as an institution, but its success may best be defined by the accomplishments of its graduates, a roster that includes suffragist Eléonore Raoul 20L, golfer Bobby Jones 29L, and IRS commissioner Randolph Thrower 36L in the school's early years. Graduates sitting on the statewide bench include Georgia Supreme Court Chief Justice Harold N. Hill Jr. 57L and Justices G. Conley Ingram 51L, P. Harris Hines 68L, and Leah Ward Sears 80L. Business executives, including former CEO of the Metropolitan Life Insurance Company C. Robert Henrikson 72L and Bacardi chairman Facundo Bacardi 96L, are also among Emory Law's alumni.

Through Emory Law's Technological Innovation: Generating Economic Results (TI:GER) program, in conjunction with Georgia Tech, law students learn the legal aspects of technology commercialization.

Leah Ward Sears 80L, chief justice of the Georgia Supreme Court from 2005 to 2009, was the first African American chief justice in the United States.

Ad astra per aspera

By Catharina Haynes 86L

Ad astra per aspera (to the stars through hardships/difficulties).

Ad astra . . .

Growing up on the space coast of Florida, it seemed as if the stars were within reach. At the age of ten, I decided my star would be a career as a lawyer, and I never looked back. I raced through high school and college and found myself, at age nineteen, showing up at Emory University Law School.

Per aspera . . .

I was excited, ambitious, and . . . totally intimidated by my impressive fellow students. Not only were they older, but also many of them had experience in the real world. As we sat there being told to "look to your right, look to your left, those people won't still be there at graduation," I resolved to aim high and be that person at graduation. So I worked hard and persevered. Three years later, I was a proud Emory Law alumna.

   Lesson learned: Don't let the abilities of others intimidate you. Work hard, persevere, aim high, and you will succeed.

Ad astra . . .

Newly minted degree in hand, I set off to Dallas to try to become a partner at a major law firm.

Per aspera . . .

I had some terrific mentors and colleagues, but I also encountered people who assumed a (very) young woman would not have what it takes. I realized that you can't let that kind of negativity get in your head. The only way to prove them wrong is to prove them wrong with excellent work. The only way to do excellent work is to work hard and challenge yourself, quieting that small voice that says, "What if I can't do it?" and just doing it. Mission accomplished: I made partner, and some of the early naysayers were among my biggest proponents.

   Lesson learned: Don't let others' low expectations define you. If you outwork everyone in the room and challenge yourself to do the very best possible, even the toughest nut can be cracked.

Ad astra . . .

So there I was in my big office looking out over the Dallas Arts District when I was approached to run for a state district judge position (Texas has partisan election of judges). Say what? Little ol' me, a judge?

Per aspera . . .

Campaigning in a county that has over a million voters is overwhelming, to say the least. I applied those long-ago lessons from Emory Law to gather support, work hard, and put my best foot forward, ending up unopposed the first go-around (the best way to run). For the next eight years, I presided over hundreds of trials and thousands of hearings, always challenging myself to follow the highest ethical standards. It was among the best eight years of my life, but after a shift in the electorate, I was not reelected to a third term. Aspera, indeed. Election night, I told myself I was going to land on my feet and that ten years later it would be the best thing that ever happened to me.

Ad astra . . .

Eighteen months later I was in New Orleans for an en banc session of the US Court of Appeals for the Fifth Circuit . . . as a member of the court!

   Lesson learned: It's not whether you are knocked down but whether you pick yourself up.

   Happy one hundredth birthday, Emory Law! Keep reaching for the stars!

The Honorable Catharina Haynes is a graduate of the Emory Law Class of 1986, where she served as an editor of the Emory Law Journal. She is a federal judge for the United States Court of Appeals for the Fifth Circuit.

The extensive network of Emory Law graduates comprises such thought leaders as the Reverend Bernice King 90L 90T, chief executive officer of the King Center. US senators Sam Nunn 62L, Wyche Fowler 69L, and Carte Goodwin 99L; state leaders such as Georgia attorney generals Sam Olens 83L and Thurbert Baker 79L; members of the US House of Representatives; US ambassadors; US District Court judges; federal and state appellate judges; and many others are also Emory Law alumni.

"We are preparing students for a lifetime as leaders, confronting problems that are unimaginable today," says Dean and Asa Griggs Candler Professor of Law Robert Schapiro. "We are preparing them for long and evolving legal careers in a changing society."

▼ ▼ ▼

At its core, the mission of Emory Law has not changed since its inception. Its founders sought to raise the caliber of the practice of law and to bring the finest legal minds to the South. "The legal profession is undoubtedly over-supplied numerically, while the demand for properly trained lawyers continues [to be] under-supplied," asserted the catalogue of the newly formed Lamar School of Law, as it was called until about 1970.

When Emory University moved its campus from rural Oxford, Georgia, to Atlanta, the creation of a law school reflected the nascent potential for the university and its city to become vanguards of the New South. The quadrangle came to life amid a seventy-five-acre wooded site known as "the Old Guess Place" in the Druid Hills neighborhood, land that

The original Emory Law building was designed by Beaux-Arts architect Henry Hornbostel and built of pink and gray Georgia marble. It was added to the National Register of Historic Places in 1975.

Emory Law's original faculty were all from Yale University's law school and used the case method for teaching their twenty-seven students.

was donated by Coca-Cola Company owner Asa Candler, who was then chairman of the university's board of trustees.

The law building resembled an Italian villa—with pink and gray Georgia marble blocks set in a quiltlike pattern, arched windows, and a terra-cotta tile roof. In 1925, the *Emory Alumnus* magazine deemed it "the most beautiful building on the campus." Many wedding couples have posed for photographs on its grand spiral staircase.

At the opening convocation on the morning of September 27, 1916, the first twenty-seven law students stood for the singing of "America" and heard inspirational words from Cone Johnson, solicitor for the US Department of State.

The full-time faculty were graduates of Yale Law School who used the case method of teaching, the Socratic style that has terrified 1Ls since it originated at Harvard Law School in the late nineteenth century.

At the time, virtually all lawyers were men, but Emory Law also opened its doors to women. Although University Chancellor Warren Candler strongly opposed coeducation, suffragist Eléonore Raoul registered in 1917 while the Methodist bishop was out of town. "When the bishop got home, it was too late. I was already in," she later recounted.

Ellyne Strickland 24L followed just a few years later and went on to practice law in Atlanta and then in Washington, DC, as part of the Internal Revenue Service legal team that prosecuted Al Capone for tax evasion.

▼ ▼ ▼

America sorely needed advances in the rule of law, but the world was in turmoil for much of the first half of the twentieth century. The nation was on the cusp of entering World War I when the Law School opened. Just twelve students enrolled in 1917, and the student body in 1918 dropped to eight. The nation's young men had joined the war effort.

Early students in the law library. At the time, the school was named for L. Q. C. Lamar, a Georgia native who served as an associate justice of the US Supreme Court.

In Emory Law's first half-century, few women followed the trailblazing path of Eléonore Raoul 20L, and the legal profession remained overwhelmingly white and male.

Emory Law soon recovered, and in 1920, in a testament to the rigor of its teaching and its admissions standards, Emory became the first law school in Georgia to gain admission to the Association of American Law Schools. In 1923, Emory received a "Class A" rating from the American Bar Association, joining the University of Virginia and Washington and Lee as one of only three law schools in the Southeast with the highest rating.

In that era, a joyful boosterism known as the "Atlanta spirit" infused the city and all its institutions. With a population of a quarter-million, Atlanta was the largest city in the Southeast, but business leaders wanted to spark even more growth. In 1925, they launched the Forward Atlanta campaign and built the city's first skyscrapers.

Beyond the Paper Chase
Building Community at Emory Law

Kaia, a Labradoodle puppy with golden fur, lies in the middle of the student commons in Gambrell Hall, as soft and still as a shag rug. Samantha Skolnick 17L gently strokes her back and neck, imagining herself back in her living room at home with her family dog.

Consider this Exhibit A of the transformation of Emory Law into a more genial place. The study of law demands hard work and inspires competition, but here students also find camaraderie, collaboration—and, occasionally, a dog or two.

Several times each semester, handlers bring dogs to offer pet therapy as a way to lower stress and lighten the mood. This kinder community prevails in other ways as well, from Thursday social gatherings in Bacardi Plaza to student participation in Emory Law Houses.

In a model borrowed from the Harry Potter stories, students are assigned to one of seven "houses" named after nearby neighborhoods, such as Druid Hills and Morningside. The houses are assigned based on legal writing sections.

They provide built-in peer support, enabling new students to lean on 2Ls and 3Ls to help them navigate the transition to law school. Each house has a signature color, and when they wear their T-shirts, the law students reflect the colors of the rainbow. "That is a very deliberate message of inclusion and diversity," says Assistant Dean Katherine Brokaw, who spearheaded development of the program.

Emory Law also has more than thirty-five student organizations, creating social networks for students to find people with similar legal perspectives (such as the American Constitution Society and Emory Federalist Society) or background (such as the Black Law Students Association and the Latin American Law Students Association).

The iconic 1973 movie *The Paper Chase* portrayed law school as a place of fear and misery, but the atmosphere at Emory Law is "the complete opposite," says Seth Park 16L 16MBA, former president of the Student Bar Association. "Just take a quick walk through the halls," he says. "You see happy people enjoying themselves. The sense of community comes across very easily."

Ethan Rosenzweig 02L, senior assistant dean for admission, financial aid, and student life, sees a central role for community in exciting students to come to Emory—and in keeping them engaged once they are here. Admitted to Emory Law as a Woodruff Scholar—a handful of students in each class who are selected based not only on their past achievements but given their capacity to be leaders at the Law School and beyond—Rosenzweig says it was the sense of community that sold him on Emory. "I felt at home at the Law School from my very first visit to campus. And I still do!"

Patricia Butler 31L was a proud graduate of Emory Law, but found it extremely difficult to find work as a woman attorney in Atlanta during the Great Depression. Years later, she made a $1 million donation to Emory Law, the largest gift ever given by a woman at that time.

These were the years when favorite Emory son Robert Tyre "Bobby" Jones Jr. captured the world stage, and a sense of pride swept Emory Law in 1930 when the famed golfer and alumnus won the Grand Slam—four major tournaments in one year—just after winning his first federal court case.

Then came the Great Depression. Emory Law stayed focused on its mission, even as it raised the standards for publication by its faculty and began offering the juris doctor (JD) degree as an alternative to the bachelor of laws (LLB). Patricia Collins Butler 31L, one of two women in her class, recalls how difficult it was to apply for law jobs during the Depression.

"In almost every case they'd say, 'Miss Collins, we'd like to hire you, we really would. But we couldn't face our clients if we told them we were paying a woman lawyer in a day when men are walking the streets, [without jobs and] with families that they have to support," she explained years later. E. Smythe Gambrell, a prominent Atlanta attorney and adjunct professor at Emory Law, worked tirelessly to help her get a job, eventually connecting her with a colleague at the US Department of Justice, where she had a long career.

The Law School inspired public service among many of its graduates. Boisfeuillet Jones 37L headed several of Atlanta's influential philanthropic foundations, and Dana Creel 34L administered several Rockefeller philanthropic funds. Hugh MacMillan 34L, a senior vice president with the Coca-Cola Export Corporation, later donated $2.3 million for the construction of a state-of-the-art law library.

When America entered World War II, Emory Law once again lost faculty and students to the nation's defense. The Law School stayed open by shifting to night classes. Enrollment surged in the postwar period, as Emory supplied young lawyers to the city's top law firms. Most veterans wore their uniforms to class while other students, mostly male, came to class in a suit and tie, taking on the demeanor of working attorneys. "You felt like you were in a place where the law was paramount," says US District Judge William C. O'Kelley 53L.

Hugh MacMillan 34L wanted Emory Law students to have a premier law library. The Hugh F. MacMillan Law Library, which opened in 1995, has a collection of about four hundred thousand volumes and volume-equivalents and a staff of ten professional law librarians.

Shuttle Diplomat between Two Schools

PHILIP S. REESE 66C 76L 76MBA

I was first accepted to Emory Law in 1966, after completing my undergraduate work at Emory, but Vietnam and a six-year tour intervened. When I reapplied in 1972, I flew from Honolulu to Atlanta and pleaded my case, and lucky for me that Bob Stubbs, the director of admissions, and Colonel Schacter, the chief administrative officer of Emory Law, were both ex-military. I think that had something to do with the school's reassessing my situation and admitting me. This was my first sign the school had some flexibility and a willingness to engineer a result.

Since my middle teens, I had liked the idea of getting both a law degree and an MBA, and indeed, many in our family went into law and then into business or politics. I was inclined toward business, a premise reinforced by my army experience running a signal company and then a signal group of four companies. The question was how.

I visited Ben Johnson, the forward-looking law dean, and asked whether he would consider the option of creating a JD/MBA program where cross credits between the two schools would permit doing in four years what might take five if done sequentially. He noted that, in fact, the faculties and administrations of both schools had already been wrestling with that issue, and he referred me to Professor Agnor, a colonel in the US Army Reserves and my real property teacher. The "Bull," as he was affectionately known to his students, connected me with Art Dietz, professor of finance and head of the MBA program at the Business School, and together we worked to convince the two schools' respective Academic Affairs Committees and the university that such a program had merit. Emory, in Agnor's opinion, only needed a "ripe issue" with which to make the case, and I became it. I withdrew from the Law School and entered the Business School with both schools knowing where I hoped this was heading. I became the shuttle diplomat between the schools over the next two years, never losing faith with Dean Johnson, who counseled, "In academia, Phil, by the inch it is a cinch, but by the yard it is hard." At the end of my third year, the program was approved and became one of the first examples of formal interdisciplinary collaboration at Emory.

Postgraduation, I joined KPMG as a tax attorney, where I readily applied both degrees, and then moved to what is now SunTrust Bank, on whose bank holding company board I now serve. In conjunction with the Alumni Association, I helped launch Career Day with Dr. Deva Scheel, where students can grill recent Emory alumni from different professions about their jobs and their companies.

It was the beginning of a long association as an alumnus, banker, energy executive, and investor that led me back to where it all had begun at Emory Law. I became chairman of the Emory Law Advisory Board and shortly after that a cochair of the Law School's most comprehensive and largest capital campaign in its history. It was then that Dean Robert Schapiro and his colleagues developed a juris master program to meet the needs of professionals from other disciplines who need grounding, not a license, in the law. Such efforts continue to this day, making Emory Law one of the most innovative law schools in the country.

Phil Reese is a 1966 graduate of Emory University and received a joint JD/MBA degree from Emory Law and what is now the Goizueta Business School in 1976. He is the retired chairman of the Delaware Public Employees Retirement System.

In 1955, the Law Alumni Association of Emory University launched a campaign dubbed "The Turning Point" to make Emory Law "one of the most outstanding law schools in the United States." They built their drive for excellence on a foundation of public service and integrity.

Sam Nunn recalls that one of his first classes was in legal ethics. "Many of the ethical principles I learned there were lessons of life that served me well during my entire career," says Nunn, who began as a lawyer in Perry, Georgia, and served twenty-four years in the US Senate.

Sam Nunn 62L was just thirty-three when he was elected to the US Senate. He served as senator from Georgia for twenty-four years.

▾ ▾ ▾

Law has never existed as something pure and separate. It is the lacework of civilization, giving structure to the messy realities of humanity. When Jonas Robitscher, a lawyer and psychiatrist, joined the Emory Law faculty in 1971, some connection between law and behavior was easy to see. But Robitscher, who was the Henry R. Luce Professor of Law and Behavioral Sciences, brought an important new perspective to the field.

He raised questions about the rights of psychiatric patients, the unbridled power of psychiatrists, and the use of forensic psychiatry in the courtroom. He invited doctors, social scientists, and lawyers to an annual Interdisciplinary Symposium in Law and the Behavioral Sciences.

Complementary disciplines again intertwined when Henry Manne joined the faculty in 1981. Manne, a bold thinker who championed free markets, was a founder of the field of law and economics and author of the seminal 1966 text *Insider Trading and the Stock Market*. He brought his Law and Economics Center to Emory to explore antitrust law, insider trading, and securities law, among other topics. "There are many areas of law where legal questions are couched in economics," he asserted. "Lawyers cannot do a responsible job without this background."

Another bold move in shaping the future of legal scholarship came in 1982. Years earlier, when Professor Frank Alexander was just an aspiring law student, James Laney, then an Emory dean, had encouraged him to pursue degrees in both law and divinity, his

John Witte Jr. is a Robert W. Woodruff Professor of Law and the McDonald Distinguished Professor. He is also director of Emory Law's Center for the Study of Law and Religion, and is a world-renowned scholar of Christian jurisprudence, marriage and family law, religious freedom, and human rights.

two seemingly dichotomous interests. When tapped as president of Emory University, Laney urged Alexander to found a groundbreaking Center for the Study of Law and Religion. With the support of Emory Law Dean Howard "Woody" Hunter, Emory Law did just that, attracting the world-renowned legal scholar Harold Berman from Harvard Law School and his protégé, John Witte Jr.

The new center encountered skepticism. What role could—or should—religious tradition play in the teaching and study of law? The center soon demonstrated not only the importance of that connection—to such issues as religious freedom and church-state relations—but also its distinct ability to bridge religious traditions and nationalities. "Law is, in many ways, the universal solvent of human living," says Witte, now a Robert W. Woodruff Professor of Law, the McDonald Distinguished Professor, and director of the Center for the Study of Law and Religion.

Under Witte's directorship since 1987, the center fosters dialogue and breaks new ground as it explores fundamental questions of human rights and religious freedom. While similar institutes have since emerged at leading universities around the world, Emory Law's center remains an interdisciplinary model with an impressive output: six degree programs, forty courses, three book series, an international journal, annual lectures and public forums, a triennial international conference, and more than three hundred books. The center has attracted more than $20 million in grant funds, including recent grants for scholarship and hands-on training in addressing issues of religious freedom and for cutting-edge scholarship on law and Christianity.

Dowd for the Defense

JOHN DOWD 65L

When I was eleven years old, I discovered the writings and trials of Clarence Darrow. I read them all and was inspired by his extraordinary advocacy of difficult and unpopular causes: religious liberty, civil rights, and the rights of the working man. He was a man of enormous intellectual breadth and depth.

Inspired by Darrow, I decided to become a criminal defense lawyer. I read *The Literature of the Law* and *The Art of Advocacy*, which contained some of the greatest trials in recorded history.

As a student at L. Q. C. Lamar School of Law at Emory, I took the full range of fundamental courses, especially civil and criminal procedure, criminal law, litigation, and legal research and writing. The requirements were rigorous, challenging, and disciplined. My legal education strengthened my ability to tackle complex legal and factual problems, and I learned the importance of being well-organized, tenacious in my research, prepared for any presentation, and always faithful to my cause. The Emory Legal Aid Society inspired me to help the less fortunate obtain fair and just treatment. Combined with my training as a US Marine officer, the rigor of Emory's legal education gave me the fundamental ingredients, confidence, and ability to deal with the most difficult, complex cases in any setting.

Over the past fifty years I have been fortunate to defend courts-martial, including capital cases and administrative proceedings. In the Department of Justice, I defended tax cases in federal and state courts, including a significant Fifth Amendment issue that went to the Supreme Court, *Couch v. United States,* 409 U.S. 322 (1973). After joining the Criminal Division, I tried Meyer Lansky and prosecuted the first criminal RICO cases, for example, *United States v. Parness,* 503 F.2d 430 (2d cir. 1974). The attorney general directed me to investigate Congressman Daniel Flood of Pennsylvania for corruption in office. Flood was indicted, convicted, and stripped of all of his power, and then I conducted the first internal investigation of the FBI of corruption by senior FBI officials, resulting in the firing of the director and associate director.

In private practice, the challenges continued, and again my background at Emory Law and in the military continued to fuel the confidence and ability to successfully take on complex cases. Several clients were public officials, including a federal judge, an assistant US Attorney, the governor of Arizona, the secretary of the treasury, and a US senator. But I was also retained as special counsel to three commissioners of Major League Baseball to conduct the investigations of Pete Rose, Don Zimmer, Lenny Dykstra, George Steinbrenner, and two umpires, and for the past ten years, I have helped our wounded veterans and their families, pro bono publico, with every conceivable legal problem. We established before the Veterans Administration that suicide resulting from PTSD and depression from experience in combat was a wound and recoverable as a death benefit for the survivors.

I have always been fully prepared to deal with these challenges—thanks to Emory Law.

And so the work goes on.

John Dowd is a graduate of the Emory Law Class of 1965. He prosecuted the first criminal RICO cases and led other prominent trials both as a prosecutor and defense attorney. As special counsel to Major League Baseball, he produced the Dowd Report, which ultimately led to Pete Rose's lifetime ban in 1989. In 2015, Dowd donated his copy of the report to the Hugh F. MacMillan Law Library.

Beyond law and religion, Berman also established a fresh and influential voice for Emory Law in the realm of legal history. In his *Law and Revolution* books, Berman asserted that the roots of Western law date to the Middle Ages and the papal revolution that freed the church from control by kings and feudal lords, rather than the much later Age of Enlightenment. His work led to a fundamental shift in thinking about the origin of the Western legal tradition.

Berman's groundbreaking work also offers a window into the broader scholarly impact of the myriad books, articles, and studies authored by the faculty of Emory Law. From constitutional law and criminal procedure to foreign relations law and financial regulation, from critical race theory and Chinese law to environmental law and education law, and from human rights and hate speech to feminism and federal jurisdiction, Emory Law scholars engage critical issues of the day, shaping the way we have thought, think today, and will think in the future about the best solutions to the world's most difficult problems.

Sam Nunn Professor of Law Frank S. Alexander founded the Center for the Study of Law and Religion at Emory Law. He served as Interim Dean of Emory Law from 2005 to 2006. He is also cofounder and senior advisor of the Center for Community Progress.

Beyond the individual contributions of its faculty, moreover, Emory Law has been a leader in shaping a number of important scholarly disciplines, including law and religion, law and economics, legal history, law and society, children's rights and family law, feminism and legal theory, and others. Particularly in those areas, but also beyond, its reach has extended yet further, in serving as a training ground for professors formerly on the faculty at Emory, but now teaching at other prestigious law schools around the nation.

As the pace of global change continues to accelerate, the law and legal education must keep up. With a commitment to innovation and scholarship, Emory Law has always been willing to adapt. "We are poised, because of our history and who we are, to respond more flexibly and creatively than most institutions," says Alexander, the Sam Nunn Professor of Law.

Outside the Classroom
*Law Clinics Bring Real-World
Experience and Lasting Impact*

When the Georgia legislature convenes every January, Emory Law students blend in with lobbyists and aides in the hallways and hearing rooms. They are tracking bills that relate to juvenile justice. In some cases, they even play a role in crafting the language of those bills.

In a signature effort that took eight years to complete, Emory Law students in the Barton Child Law and Policy Center worked with stakeholders and legislators to rewrite the state's juvenile code, revisions that passed the legislature in 2013.

"It represents a shared public agenda for what justice for youth is and should be," says Melissa Carter, executive director of the center. The project placed Emory Law "at the forefront of policy-making in the state," she says.

The Barton Center is just one way that Emory Law students gain hands-on experience working with clients and addressing issues of public policy. Emory Law has three clinics within the Barton Center and three focused on other legal areas: the Barton Center Appeal for Youth Clinic, the Barton Center Juvenile Defender Clinic, the Barton Center Policy and Legislative Clinic, the International Humanitarian Law Clinic, the Turner Environmental Law Clinic, and the Volunteer Clinic for Veterans.

*The Barton Child Law and Policy Center
advocates for children in the child
welfare and juvenile justice systems*

♥ ♥ ♥

Two young associates sit across from their new "client," Casey Schultz, the mother of a teenage tennis phenomenon so explosive on the court that he is known as "Kid Dynamite." Schultz has been fielding offers to license "Kid Dynamite" as a brand of tennis rackets and clothing, and the lawyers assure her they're going to get her the best deal possible.

But first, they need a sense of what she thinks would be a good deal. They probe with their talking points. She's willing to take a little bit less in royalties to get the deal nailed down quickly. "We're really anxious to capitalize on this opportunity," says Schultz, aka Katherine Koops, assistant director of the Emory Law Center for Transactional Law and Practice.

There are possible pitfalls—questions about what might be expected from her son's performance on and off the court—and a potential upside if he catches fire as both a player and a brand. In another room nearby, their counterparts are meeting with an executive of Sports Heroes Licensing Company, aka Susan Kolodkin, an adjunct professor.

At the end of the three weeks of negotiations, the most tangible outcome will be one that none of the parties will directly address: a grade. This exercise in transactional law is yet another example of continued innovation in the Emory Law curriculum.

"We're trying to help students understand how to translate the theory and doctrine of contracts into serving clients and constructing documents that protect their interests," says Charles Howard Candler Professor of Law Emeritus William Carney, founder of the skills-based transactional program, which began in 2007. He and his wife later donated $1 million in matching funds to be used to strengthen the program.

Carney helped recruit Tina Stark, a pioneer in transactional skills training, as the first director. The program evolved into a full curriculum that enables students to obtain a Transactional Law Certificate.

Moving from textbooks to the negotiating table, constructing closing documents for a merger or acquisition, learning about venture

A pioneer in transactional skills training, Tina Stark developed the curriculum enabling law students to earn a special certificate in the field.

capital—those were once unheard-of concepts in legal education. But today, about two hundred Emory Law students take at least the foundational courses of the transactional law program each year.

"They learn how to talk to a client, how to talk about a deal, and how that's different from talking about litigation," says Sue Payne, a former corporate lawyer who is now executive director of the Center for Transactional Law and Practice. "It's a different way of asking questions and a different way of listening."

Experiential education has become an increasingly important part of law school programs across the country. In 2015, the American Bar Association added a minimum requirement for experiential coursework, but Emory Law students already far exceeded that standard.

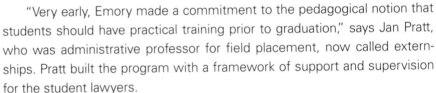

"Very early, Emory made a commitment to the pedagogical notion that students should have practical training prior to graduation." —*Jan Pratt*

"Very early, Emory made a commitment to the pedagogical notion that students should have practical training prior to graduation," says Jan Pratt, who was administrative professor for field placement, now called externships. Pratt built the program with a framework of support and supervision for the student lawyers.

Today, about 80 percent of students participate in a clinic or take an externship, gaining legal experience in a nonprofit, governmental, or corporate legal environment. All 2Ls are required to participate in the Kessler-Eidson Program for Trial Techniques, and students gain practical training through simulation exercises in transactional law and trial advocacy courses, among others. Student practice societies, another unique aspect of the Emory Law program, are designed to mirror distinct areas of legal practice, giving students a chance to learn about their chosen specialties and to network with alumni.

As the practice of law has become more specialized, so has the Emory Law curriculum. Emory Law students are better prepared than ever before to enter the profession. "We have been incredibly focused on building the breadth and depth of the curriculum," says Vice Dean Robert Ahdieh. "No matter their field of interest, every Emory Law student can now graduate ready to add value from day one." ♥

Jan Pratt built the externship program at Emory Law that provides a framework of support and supervision for the students.

Professor Sue Payne, a former corporate lawyer, is executive director of Emory Law's Center for Transactional Law and Practice, an innovative program that has become a national model.

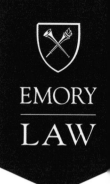

CHAPTER TWO

Challenging the Status Quo

The winter sun streams through the wall of windows of Hunter Atrium in Gambrell Hall, a strong and clear light that belies the briskness of the cold air outside. Here, the air is heated with righteous indignation.

Somber images linger on a large pull-down screen, a silent display punctuated by the sound of gunshots: John Jr. saluting at the funeral of his father, President John F. Kennedy. Girls sobbing after the massacre at Columbine High School in Colorado. White balloons in memory of the victims of the shooting at Sandy Hook Elementary School in Connecticut.

The images form a backdrop for objections to a pivotal US Supreme Court case on the Second Amendment, presented through the dramatic reading of a play crafted by longtime professor Frank Vandall, who advocates for regulation on access to guns.

At that same moment, in a different part of the building, a more serene conversation centers on natural law, the inherent rights of all human beings. The speakers reflect on the perspective of four religions: Christianity, Judaism, Islam, and Hinduism. Elsewhere, students emerge from a class where they have discussed the delicate balance of security and privacy, the outgrowth of an age of terrorism.

On any given day, Emory Law is a place of thoughtful debate, of unconventional ideas, of argument and counterargument. Theory moves into a real-world context in pioneering ways—for example, through the student-run Supreme Court Advocacy Program, which secured a grant of certiorari to the US Supreme Court in 2012 in a bankruptcy case, which it ultimately won in a unanimous decision; through the student-run bankruptcy law journal, the only one of its kind in the country; and through innovative legal clinics, which helped rewrite Georgia's juvenile code and train military and civilian leaders in the law of armed conflict.

"Our students are exposed to the practice of law in ways that don't happen everywhere else."

— Vice Dean Robert Ahdieh

"Our students are exposed to the practice of law in ways that don't happen everywhere else," says Vice Dean Robert Ahdieh, who is also K. H. Gyr Professor of Private International Law.

◆ ◆ ◆

Having a vibrant discussion requires a mix of voices. Emory draws its faculty and students from around the country and the world. It seeks diversity of every type—of ideas, geography, ethnic and racial background, and sexual orientation and gender identity.

Vice Dean Robert Ahdieh is K. H. Gyr Professor of Private International Law. He is a leading scholar in international financial regulation and trade.

From Living in Poverty to Living the Dream

MOLLY HILAND PARMER 12L

For me, law school was supposed to be a pipe dream. It was supposed to remain a wistful, lofty ambition, one that required too much time and certainly too much money to ever seriously consider. And to study law at a prestigious private school still seems so far beyond the bounds of my reality that, even now, having graduated from Emory University School of Law, things still seem dreamlike.

According to recent statistics, one out of every three children in America lives in poverty. Though growing up in poverty certainly does not preclude one from having a good childhood or a loving childhood, like many in this country, I did grow up very poor. I also grew up in a rather nontraditional setting, the lovechild of a couple of countercultural hippies. My dad was an artist, renowned for illustrating Abbie Hoffman's *Steal This Book* and being a psychedelic cartoonist extraordinaire. My mother was a feminist, a free spirit, and by all accounts, an excellent mother to my sisters and me. On one hand, my life was colorful and bohemian. There were paintings and art supplies everywhere; my mom sewed our clothes, backpacks, and bedding; we'd eat from giant batches of "peasant food," as my dad called it, one-pot meals that would last for a week and feed plenty. On the other hand, my life was limited. Getting injured did not mean I went to the doctor; a holiday did not mean gifts; and afternoons and weekends were spent not with friends but working part-time jobs so that I would have enough money for class field trips and orthodontic braces.

I can't pinpoint exactly how or why I started seriously considering law school. It was a combination of many things that led me to study for the LSAT and begin the application process. But I can pinpoint exactly when I knew that I would be able to attend law school. It wasn't after my applications were submitted or when acceptances started rolling in. It was the moment I got a phone call from the admissions office at Emory Law, telling me that I was offered the Woodruff Fellowship and could attend law school tuition-free, with a stipend every semester.

Emory Law created incredible opportunities for me. Unsurprisingly, I chose to be an advocate for the indigent. After graduation, I spent three years working as a county public defender. Currently, I work as an assistant federal defender. I am honored to work for incredible leaders in indigent defense, pillars of the legal community who share my alma mater: Claudia Saari 87L, the chief public defender of DeKalb County, and now, Stephanie Kearns 75L, federal defender for the Northern District of Georgia.

Emory Law changed my dream into reality. It turned a girl with a homemade wardrobe and no cash for school field trips into a lawyer with a degree from a renowned institution, arguing before the Eleventh Circuit, and trying cases before federal district judges. It provided me with a comfortable home, money to pay the bills each month, and the opportunity to use a powerful degree to help those most in need. For me, Emory University School of Law changed living in poverty to living the dream.

Molly Hiland Parmer is a graduate of the Emory Law Class of 2012. She is assistant federal defender for the Federal Defender Program for the Northern District of Georgia, based in Atlanta.

At the Intersection of Law and Global Health

Polly Price 86C 86G

As the recent Ebola epidemic in West Africa made clear, the need for a coherent system of global health law and governance has never been greater, and much of the guidance in this arena comes from Emory Law.

In 1995, we offered our first joint degree program in law

The Global Health Law and Policy Project provides a unique multidisciplinary platform for developing, exploring, and evaluating global health initiatives.

and public health, the JD/MPH. Shortly afterward, we began collaborating with the prestigious Emory University Rollins School of Public Health and the world-renowned Centers for Disease Control and Prevention (CDC) to provide groundbreaking programs in global public health law.

Now, in addition to the JD/MPH, Emory Law offers a JD/MA in bioethics, where health policy and law intersect, and we also boast our newest degree program, the juris master, which offers a concentration in global public health law.

The Global Health Law and Policy Project provides a unique multidisciplinary platform for developing, exploring, and evaluating global health initiatives. Our location in Atlanta offers students extraordinary access to institutions in public

health, including the CDC, located on Emory's campus; influential clinics and policy centers through Emory Healthcare; and the Carter Center, an Emory affiliate.

These various programs have allowed Emory Law to have a measurable impact on contemporary global health challenges by drawing on the university's diverse strengths in law, health care, business, liberal arts, and social sciences. Such programs enable us to provide a forum for students and scholars to address global health law and policy issues, including hands-on student practicum experiences and research in global health law and policy. Numerous students over the years have served as interns at the CDC as well as at the World Health Organization in Geneva, Switzerland. The near-term future is equally promising as we focus on adding expertise in regulatory issues, the legal dimensions of health insurance and business, and how these subjects influence international developments.

Polly J. Price graduated from Emory University in 1986 with her bachelor of arts and master of arts degrees. She holds joint appointments at Emory Law and the Rollins School of Public Health as professor of law and professor of global health.

Almost 30 percent of the student body is from a minority group, and nearly two hundred students are international. Emory was one of the first universities in the country to establish an Office of LGBT Life, and the Emory OUTLaw chapter fosters a supportive community and advocates for LGBTQ issues. In 2016, the Black Law Students Association was named National BLSA Large Chapter of the Year. The honor, given to one of two hundred chapters around the country, was a first for Emory Law's BLSA.

Commitment to diversity is always a work in progress. Emory Law recruits a diverse population and offers significant scholarships to support those efforts. Current students and alumni are important partners in that outreach. Gwen Keyes Fleming 93L pushed for greater diversity recruitment when she was vice president of the BLSA. Now she is a role model for breaking barriers: the first African American woman to serve as solicitor general and later district attorney in DeKalb County, Georgia, and as regional administrator of the Environmental Protection Agency in the Southeast.

Gwen Keyes Fleming 93L, principal legal adviser for US Immigration and Customs Enforcement, is a role model for breaking barriers.

"To be a global leader, Emory needs to grow and nurture lawyers who are going to be able to speak to all communities, regardless of where they are in the world or across the country, and appreciate and understand the diverse communities we're going to be representing," says Fleming, who is now principal legal adviser for Immigration and Customs Enforcement

continued on page 35

The Legacy of Eléonore Raoul 20L

Emory Law Explores the Role of Gender— and All Human Vulnerability

Ah, you were heroines all, dear, blessed heroines. You were victorious conquerors over human prejudice and ignorance.

> —Letter from Carrie Chapman Catt, president of the National American Woman Suffrage Association, to Eléonore Raoul 20L and other suffragists, after the ratification of the Nineteenth Amendment

Emory's first woman law student, Eléonore Raoul 20L.

A year before Eléonore Raoul became the first woman at Emory Law, she journeyed through the glass-making panhandle region of West Virginia, armed with Bible verses, jokes, and talking points about women's suffrage. Her greatest challenge was to control her passion and temper in the face of vehement opposition to that state's 1916 referendum on women's suffrage.

"The latest thing is not to have publicity about the real work because the antis get on to it and counteract the suffrage influence," she wrote to her sister, Rosine. "And it is really hard not to let things get out. They leak out in the most unaccountable manner."

Over the course of her career, Raoul found many routes to advancing the role of women. In 1917, she became the first woman to enroll at Emory Law, while still pressing for women's suffrage. She founded the Central Committee of Women Citizens, the forerunner of the Atlanta League of Women Voters, when women won the right to vote in Atlanta municipal primary elections in 1919. The Nineteenth Amendment to the US Constitution was ratified just before Raoul began her final year of law school in 1920.

"I went into suffrage because I thought it was just and that it was the most effective way for women to uphold their chief interests—the home and children," said Raoul,

> "I went into suffrage because I thought it was just and that it was the most effective way for women to uphold their chief interests—the home and children," said Raoul, who did not change her name after marrying an Emory Law classmate in 1928. "Women's interests must be represented in government."
>
> *—Eléonore Raoul*

who did not change her name after marrying an Emory Law classmate in 1928. "Women's interests must be represented in government."

Today's young women could hardly imagine the world of Eléonore Raoul, but in many ways she laid the groundwork for future progressive action. "Women's interests" formed the basis of the Feminism and Legal Theory Project, which Martha Albertson Fineman, Robert W. Woodruff Professor of Law, brought to Emory in 2004. The project explores the impact of laws as they relate to gender. That focus encompasses reproductive rights, employment, poverty, and family law. The project also holds symposia on such topics as sexuality and single mothers and the sometimes competing claims of children's rights and family privacy.

Fineman has always been interested not just in the rule of law but in the impact of law on society. In 2008, she moved the focus of the project beyond gender to look at how all people can be disadvantaged in various ways—problems that are not resolved merely by creating gender-neutral laws.

"We used to think of the work-family conflict as a gender issue because we assumed all caretakers were women," she says. "But it isn't the gender of the caretaker that's the issue. The problem is that this society does not value caretakers."

Over the course of her prolific career,

Robert W. Woodruff Professor of Law Martha Albertson Fineman.

Emory Law honors exceptional alumnae with the Eléonore Raoul Trailblazer Award.

Fineman has been a major influence on law and society, as well as on critical legal theory, which challenges the concept that law is neutral and examines the ways in which laws perpetuate injustice.

Her latest project, the Vulnerability and the Human Condition Initiative, explores shared vulnerability as a universal and constant aspect of the human condition, considering the ways that law and policies shape social conditions and practices in areas such as poverty, social welfare, and the market economy. The initiative focuses on social justice and the institutions and organization of society, arguing for a responsive state more attentive to human needs.

Fineman appreciates the pathways that have already been forged, which enable this much deeper discussion—and she is aware of the difficulty of change. "I've seen a lot of change over the course of my career, but I also see a lot of backlash and pushback," she says. "It worries me how quickly things can be undone if you lose sight of the history of struggle and the need to continue to fight for progress."

Helping to Attract the Best

ROBERT HENRIKSON 72L

As an alumnus of Emory Law, one of my greatest passions has been promoting diversity at the school, and one way I've enjoyed doing that is by providing scholarship assistance for incoming students. In order to share how this passion developed, I thought I should explain how I became a law student and how I came to realize the importance of diverse viewpoints and backgrounds in the workplace.

In 1969, I was a senior English literature major from Alabama attending the University of Pennsylvania. I had no idea what my next steps could or should be—and I wasn't driven by any particular passion to decide. One day, a letter appeared in my mailbox in my father's unmistakable, beautiful engineer's handwriting. I was surprised. A collect phone call on Sundays was our normal mode of communication.

In the letter, he asked if I had planned my steps following graduation. Would I go to graduate school? If not, he wanted me to know that he had a friend who owned a construction company in Montreal. I had a job in Canada if I wanted it! My dad—a Pacific Theatre US Army World War II vet—was worried about Vietnam and about his son. It was an emotional moment for me. I called home immediately to tell him how much this offer meant to me. No, I would not be choosing Canada, but admittedly I was still aimless.

He then asked, "Why don't you go to law school?" I thought, "Why not?" I applied to several schools in the Southeast, was accepted at all, and chose Emory.

What's the point of this story? It's this: I wish I could say I went to law school because of my passion for the law or as a result of a burning desire to practice. I went merely because I could. That's not a particularly admirable reason, but it illustrates how accessibility can define the composition of our study body.

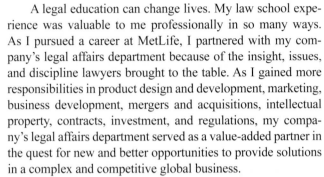

A legal education can change lives. My law school experience was valuable to me professionally in so many ways. As I pursued a career at MetLife, I partnered with my company's legal affairs department because of the insight, issues, and discipline lawyers brought to the table. As I gained more responsibilities in product design and development, marketing, business development, mergers and acquisitions, intellectual property, contracts, investment, and regulations, my company's legal affairs department served as a value-added partner in the quest for new and better opportunities to provide solutions in a complex and competitive global business.

Throughout my career, I observed time and time again that when I compared the work of two equally talented teams, the team whose members looked and thought alike almost always lost to the team where the members were diverse in their ideas, their way of doing things, and their perspectives. The diverse team always created and provided better winning solutions for their customers.

Similarly, to be successful, law firms and legal affairs departments must be as diverse in their thinking as their clients and customers. Demand for diverse talent in the legal profession is greater than ever—and growing.

Like all top law schools, Emory Law competes for the best students. But some of these students are discouraged from attending Emory because of the cost. Scholarships focused on furthering diversity help make law school accessible to more people and pave the way for us to bring together talented, qualified, and passionate students—students who help make Emory Law one of the best law schools in the country.

I want Emory Law to continue to grow its reputation and position in the global legal community. Cost should never be the factor that precludes us from attracting the best and brightest. For me, paying it forward through scholarships has an exponential impact. When Emory Law attracts and retains diverse, passionate students, the Law School is strengthened.

C. Robert Henrikson is a graduate of the Emory Law Class of 1972 and is former CEO and chairman of MetLife Insurance.

continued from page 31

at the US Department of Homeland Security.

The path to broader access began in 1961, when integration was a highly combustible topic in the South. Sit-ins by students from Emory and other local colleges helped force the integration of Atlanta's lunch counters, as marches, boycotts, and other civil rights protests spread across the South.

Newly appointed dean Ben Johnson Jr. 40L wanted Emory Law to gain prominence as one of the nation's great law schools, and that would require attracting the best and brightest students, regardless of race or gender. "My father was convinced the South would not flourish with segregation and

that Emory would not achieve a great university or law school if it did not fight against segregated society," said Ben Johnson III 64C 14H, who served eighteen years on the Emory University Board of Trustees, thirteen of them as chair.

Emory's charter and bylaws contained no restrictive language, but there was one daunting issue: A private school in Georgia could be at risk of losing its tax-exempt status if it integrated.

Johnson, an expert in tax law, and Henry L. Bowden 34L, chair of the board of trustees, sued the state, pointing out a contradiction in the law. The Georgia Constitution required private schools to be open to the "general public" in order to receive tax-exempt status. Yet it also required them to be segregated to qualify for an exemption—a clear restriction on admissions. Johnson and Bowden also argued that the segregation requirement violated the equal

Ben F. Johnson III 64C 14H was a longtime chairman of the Emory University Board of Trustees, as well as son of former Emory Law dean Ben Johnson Jr. 40L.

protection clause of the Fourteenth Amendment of the US Constitution.

In 1962, in *Emory v. Nash*, the Georgia Supreme Court agreed that those two provisions were in "irreconcilable conflict" and declared that Emory—and any private school in the state—could integrate without losing its tax-exempt status.

⚜ ⚜ ⚜

Ted Smith 65L became the first black student at Emory Law when he enrolled in the program in the fall of 1963. But Johnson's vision of an integrated Law School remained elusive.

One day in the late summer of 1965, as Marvin Arrington 67L was getting ready to return for his second year at Howard University School of Law in Washington, DC, he decided to visit Emory Law. Ben Johnson spotted him, invited him into his office, and asked if he might be interested in transferring. "I don't know," Arrington later recalled saying. "But I'll think about it and I'll get back to you."

Arrington immediately went to his friend and fellow Howard Law student Clarence Cooper 67L and convinced him to come, too. This was a chance not only to attend a prestigious school but to be on the forefront of integration. Arrington went on to found one of the leading black law firms in America,

The enrollment of Ted Smith 65L paved the way for the diversity that has become integral to the Emory Law community.

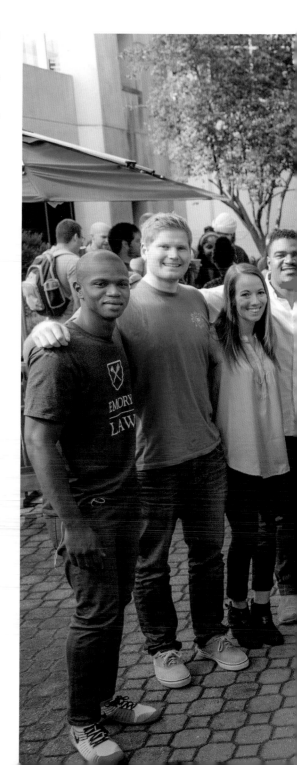

HOWARD O. HUNTER ATRIUM

2016–17 Emory Law Student Bar Association Leaders.

become president of the Atlanta City Council, and serve as a Fulton County Superior Court judge. Cooper is a senior US District Judge.

Johnson also wanted to bring more women into a field that was still almost completely male. One Friday afternoon in the fall of 1963, Lucy McGough was gazing at the bulletin board in the Law School, where her brother was a student. She was beginning to doubt her path as an Emory doctoral student in English. Johnson came out of his office and asked if she was interested in studying law. When she said yes, they talked some more, and he invited her to enter that semester. "I'll have to call my dad and see if I can get the money," she recalls saying. "He said, 'Well, we can work with you on that.'" McGough started the next Monday.

Creating a racially diverse community at Emory Law was more complicated than just opening the doors. Johnson was convinced that the prevailing admission criteria did not fairly reflect how well African American students could perform in law school, if given the chance. With support from the Field Foundation in Chicago, Emory Law was able to craft a new approach.

The Pre-Start Program, directed by Professor Michael DeVito, relied on advisers at historically black colleges and universities to identify promising candidates who would not qualify under normal admission criteria. Those students would take a ten-week summer session on torts, and if they received a passing grade, they would be admitted to the Law School. They also received financial assistance.

On the Vanguard of Change
Those Who Broke Barriers Are Now Legacies

When Judge Glenda Hatchett 77L walked over to the table of admitted students at the Black Law Students Association reception, she sparked a celebrity moment. Prospective students gathered around her for selfies.

But that moment was significant in a different way for Hatchett. She was truly happy to meet the bright and enthusiastic students. "It really gratifies me to come back and see such a diverse population at Emory," she said.

Hatchett doled out tough love and justice on her Emmy-nominated courtroom television show from 2000 to 2009. Today, she has a national law firm and a new television show.

But in the mid-1970s, Hatchett was a regional representative of BLSA, striving to recruit black law students to Emory Law. She later became the first African American to serve as chief judge of the juvenile court in Fulton County, Georgia, still working to break barriers.

Emory Law helps shape the future of the legal profession, she says. "It is important that we look like the world we seek to serve."

Judge Thelma Wyatt Cummings Moore 71L was among the first African American women to enroll at the Law School. She recalls that some classmates initially did not want her as a study partner—but success was her vindication. She ultimately graduated with distinction and was a member of the Order of the Coif honor society.

She went on to attain many more firsts: First woman to serve full-time as an Atlanta Municipal Court and City Court judge, first woman to serve as chief judge of the Superior Court of Fulton County, first African American woman to serve as a judge on the State Courts of Georgia, and first African American woman to serve as chief administrative judge in any Georgia judicial circuit.

"Be aware that people who have gone before have carved the path that you now travel," she told the BLSA students in a keynote address. "Be grateful that the path has been carved for you."

Many of those trailblazers are now legacies—parents of Emory Law students or alumni. Hatchett's son graduated in 2001. Judge Marvin Arrington Sr. 67L was one of the first African American students at Emory Law; his son Marvin Jr. 96L, niece Jill 95L, and nephew Joseph II 96L all are Emory Law alumni.

"The legacy opportunity is new for people of color," says Gwen Keyes Fleming. "They have had phenomenal careers, and they want that same opportunity for their children."

That legacy has enriched Emory Law. In 2016, the Emory Law BLSA was named national large chapter of the year. A slideshow at the reception highlighted the chapter's energy and engagement, a year's worth of activities that included charitable events, blood drives, voter registration, networking, and a lecture series. BLSA president Jewel Quintyne 16L urged prospective students in attendance to add to that trajectory. "I hope you come to experience this family that we have created here," she said.

Thelma Wyatt Cummings Moore 71L

Emory Law participants at the finals of a Law Day moot court competition in 1969. Left to right: Alfred Roach Jr 69L, Hon. Stanley F. Birch Jr. 70L 76L, John "Sonny" Morris 69L, Col. William T. Snyder, USAF 69L, Lynn R. Battle 70L.

Twelve students, including five women, entered the first Pre-Start Program in 1966. Nine of them successfully completed the summer session, and with the exception of one who dropped out to get married, they all finished their first year. By 1971, forty-one students had gained admission to Emory Law through Pre-Start. Eighteen had graduated, nine were current students, two transferred to other law schools, and fourteen withdrew.

"[Pre-Start] has been recognized as more than a gesture," Johnson wrote in his first report to the Field Foundation. "It has been seen, and embraced, as a positive, good-faith effort to work at correcting a situation which is injurious to every aspect of our society."

Two years later, Pre-Start became the model for a national program called the Council on Legal Education Opportunity (CLEO). Enrollment of African American students grew; the class of 1969 included Sanford Bishop, who later became a US congressman from Middle and Southwest Georgia.

As social change swept the nation, Emory Law was at the forefront of broadening the legal profession. "We were trying to increase not just the number of black students at Emory but the number of black lawyers in America," says Professor Nathaniel Gozansky, now emeritus, who served as director of CLEO from 1970 to 1972. "And our efforts, combined with those of others, worked."

> **"[Pre-Start] has been recognized as more than a gesture. It has been seen, and embraced, as a positive, good-faith effort to work at correcting a situation which is injurious to every aspect of our society."**
>
> **—Dean Ben Johnson Jr.**

▼ ▼ ▼

Emory Law likewise sought to nurture a sense of duty to serve the public among its students. In the 1950s, the school offered credit for working at the Atlanta Legal Aid Society, which had been founded by several local attorneys, including prominent lawyer and early Emory Law faculty member E. Smythe Gambrell. Additionally, during Johnson's tenure, Emory Law required students to complete a minimum of thirty hours of public service.

In 1967, Emory Law secured a grant from the federal Office of Economic Opportunity to launch the Emory Community Legal Services Center, with one office at the Law School and another in a low-income community. Maynard Jackson, who would become the city's first African American mayor just six years later, directed the office in the Bedford Pines neighborhood, supervising students as they resolved disputes and helped residents avoid eviction.

In 1967, assistant professor Frederic LeClercq and Dean Ben Johnson opened the Emory Community Legal Services Center on Oxford Road.

"We are convinced that if low-income people have access to high-quality legal talent they will turn to the law rather than the streets as a means of processing their individual grievances and promoting institutional change," Frederic LeClercq, an assistant professor and center director, told reporters at the time.

Gozansky, then a new professor, set up video recordings of third-year law students working with clients—a novel technique long before such technology became simple and inexpensive. The offices were a laboratory for teaching the skills of interviewing and counseling clients. Law students represented juvenile offenders and provided free research and advice through the Emory Legal Assistance for Inmates Program.

In 1968, Emory Law students took on a project much larger than any individual grievance or hardship. For years, heavy rains had sent the city's sewage flushing through Proctor Creek, overflowing into homes and washing away backyards in an impoverished African American community. Five children had drowned in the flash floods. Emory Law saw it as a case of environmental injustice.

Emory Law students researched the law, attended neighborhood meetings, and filed a class-action suit against the city. Residents planned a march on city hall—until suddenly the city came up with fifty thousand dollars to address the flooding. The lawsuit led to an agreement by the city to revamp its storm water and sewage system.

The Legal Services Center eventually closed as Atlanta Legal Aid became more robust. But the work that began under Dean Ben Johnson created the framework for the hands-on training and public service that are at the heart of the Law School today, including clinics that provide legal representation for juveniles and veterans. The public service requirement was dropped, but the students remain committed to the ideal of public service, and students who complete twenty-five hours per year of pro bono work receive recognition at graduation. In 2015, Emory Law underscored its commitment in this area by creating a new deanship for public service, naming Hunton & Williams's pro bono partner Rita Sheffey to the position. Sheffey supports students interested in careers in government or public interest law and advises the Emory Public Interest Committee, which offers grants that enable students to take unpaid summer positions.

My Emory Experience

PATRISE PERKINS-HOOKER 84MBA 84L

I am very proud of my Emory Law education and how my training prepared me for my career and my work to benefit others. I was in the first wave of students to pursue a law degree in conjunction with another degree, obtaining both an MBA and a JD through simultaneous coursework at both colleges in 1984. The training I received has been vital to my professional successes. When I left law school, I had expertise in accounting, taxation, real estate, and business transactions, which allowed me to obtain employment with a national public accounting firm and to work in the commercial real estate department of a law firm. I have had unique career options that would not have been possible without the courses that provided me the fundamentals I needed.

I have been in my own private practice, partner in charge of the commercial real estate section at a law firm, general counsel of the Atlanta BeltLine (one of the most transformative projects in Atlanta's history), and in 2016 was selected unanimously by the Fulton County Board of Commissioners to be the county attorney.

While attending Emory, I was also nurtured in an environment that fostered opportunities for me to be a leader of my peers, whether president of the JD/MBA Association or being elected president of the Gate City Bar Association in 1996 and the first African American president of the State Bar of Georgia. Along the way, I was inducted into the Gate City Bar Association's Hall of Fame, and was also awarded the Amicus Curiae award from the Georgia Supreme Court and the Eléonore Raoul Greene Trailblazer Award from Emory Law.

Emory Law provided me the legal skills to assist others in the Atlanta community, such as helping with issues impacting the sexual exploitation of minors, hunger, homelessness, and affordable housing. I consider myself fortunate to have been the attorney to lead what is now known as Youth Spark, the first-of-its-kind shelter for teenage girls who have been sexually exploited, and to have developed legislation increasing criminal penalties for pimps associated with abusive activities toward young people. Emory's commitment to and focus on public service exposed me to myriad ways that lawyers can serve their communities, and its environment allowed me the opportunity to find my own ways to serve.

Emory is the type of law school that takes high-aspiring young people and provides them with the tools to be future leaders. I am proud to be one of its alumni.

Patrise Perkins-Hooker is a 1984 graduate of Emory Law and Goizueta Business School. She is the county attorney for Fulton County, Georgia.

The Pro Bono Publico award, given at graduation, honors law students nationwide for their contributions of pro bono service to the profession.

E. Smythe Gambrell donated one million dollars for the construction of a new Law School building, and at its dedication in 1973, he remarked, "It is not difficult to understand that for many reasons this law school in Atlanta, Georgia, has a unique opportunity and a unique responsibility to serve as a legal lighthouse for the entire South."

Today, that vision has no boundaries, as Emory Law extends its reach nationally and even globally. Challenging the status quo and striving for the public good remain central to the Emory Law mission.

♦ ♦ ♦

Geoffrey Fettus, a senior attorney at the Natural Resources Defense Council (NRDC), stands at the podium in an Emory Law classroom and begins his argument. "Good morning, and may it please the court . . ."

The moot court, that is. About ten students from the Turner Environmental Law Clinic helped draft briefs on parts of this complex case, and now they are listening as the lead attorney representing environmental groups from around the country prepares for an argument before the US Court of Appeals for the DC Circuit.

The NRDC and nine other environmental groups successfully sued the Nuclear Regulatory Commission (NRC) over its rule allowing spent nuclear fuel rods to be stored indefinitely at nuclear plants. There is no federal disposal site for nuclear waste, and the environmental groups asserted that the NRC failed to consider the environmental impact or possible alternatives to such storage, as required by law.

Now the NRC has issued an environmental analysis that environmental groups consider woefully inadequate. The case is back before the appeals court.

Martin Blunt 14L, one of the student cofounders of the Volunteer Clinic for Veterans, received the Nineteenth Annual PSJD Pro Bono Publico Award for his efforts with the clinic. The annual award honors one law student nationwide for pro bono contributions to society. PSJD is the Public Service Jobs Directory administered by the National Association for Legal Career Professionals (NALP).

"Is this all just a hidden policy argument? Are we really just trying to end nuclear licensing?" asks Shelby Hancock 17L, who became so consumed by the complicated case in the fall semester that she returned to the moot court arguments although she was no longer in the clinic. "Aren't we asking the court to do Congress's job?"

"No, Your Honor, this is not a policy argument. This is not about stopping nuclear licensing," Fettus responds. "We hope this will inform a more meaningful realization—by agencies, by Congress, by the public—of what this licensing means."

The questions go on, mirroring the possible holes the judges might probe in the argument, scheduled to take place in just a few weeks. Every year, the Turner Environmental Law Clinic provides more than four thousand hours of pro bono legal work toward three goals: promoting clean and sustainable energy, supporting sustainable and urban agriculture, and protecting natural resources.

Another goal, of course, is to graduate young lawyers with a passion for carrying on good work. "We hope this is inspiring to you, and that this makes you interested in doing this kind of work," Diane Curran, another environmental attorney working on the NRC case, told the students, "because the world needs environmental lawyers to fight for a better planet." ♥

Led by Professor Mindy Goldstein, the Turner Environmental Law Clinic provides more than four thousand hours annually of pro bono legal work promoting clean energy, supporting sustainable urban agriculture, and protecting natural resources.

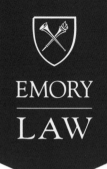

CHAPTER THREE

Reaching beyond Boundaries

Considering the circumstances, the negotiations were going well. Strained politeness prevailed. No one interrupted. No one exploded in anger. No one walked out.

On that day in Syria, Russian air strikes hit two hospitals and a school in northern towns held by rebel groups, although Russia and other world powers had been working toward a temporary halt in fighting. Thousands of miles away, however, in an Emory Law seminar room, the dignity of international law prevailed as UN representatives brought together backers of Syrian president Bashar Assad and opposition leaders.

Former US president Jimmy Carter spent many years at Emory Law coteaching Advanced International Negotiation with Professor Paul Zwier. He continues to speak at Emory's International Student Forum.

EMORY

So far, Assad's negotiators had insisted on sticking with Syria's 2012 constitution, but had agreed to allow some changes. The parties discussed moving swiftly to new elections. But things got testy when an opposition leader insisted that Assad must step down and the International Criminal Court must consider evidence of war crimes.

It was time for a professorial reality check: "You shortcut a lot of issues," cautioned Tom Crick, associate director of the Carter Center's Conflict Resolution Program, who coteaches Advanced International Negotiation with Professor Paul Zwier. He noted that a constitutional convention would probably precede elections. "The challenge is to get away from an imperial presidency."

The nine students around the conference table come from different nationalities and backgrounds, but they share a passion for international law. In this class, they move weekly through some of the most intractable conflicts in the world, including those in Sudan, Somalia, and Liberia.

The nine students around the conference table come from different nationalities and backgrounds, but they share a passion for international law. In this class, they move weekly through some of the most intractable conflicts in the world, including those in Sudan, Somalia, and Liberia. They not only learn about the work of the Carter Center, but they have the rare opportunity to bring their youthful voices and ideas to someone working on restoring peace.

"We can have issues aired in a safe environment that are the same issues that people are wrestling with in diplomatic circles today," says Crick.

Emory Law inspires students to apply the rule of law to the pressing problems of the day, and students rise to the challenge. They have researched UN resolutions on sexual orientation and gender identity; debated the issues underlying the 2014 protests in Ferguson, Missouri; and handled intellectual property concerns for technology startups.

Legal education once focused almost exclusively on the mastery of litigation skills and the foundations of case law. Today, Emory Law prepares students to thrive in a globally connected and rapidly changing environment. It is a proving ground for young lawyers who will make a difference in their cities, their nation, and the world.

▼ ▼ ▼

Long before the dawn of this millennium, Emory Law set out a broad vision, one that invited a global exchange of ideas, scholars, and students. Today, an international perspective runs through the curriculum. A family lawyer might need to consider immigration issues. A criminal defense lawyer may encounter questions of extradition. A transactional lawyer may deal with companies based overseas. A public health lawyer may consider global travel restrictions and quarantine in the face of communicable diseases.

Unique among law schools, students in the Emory Law International Humanitarian Law Clinic provide support for human rights organizations.

"For every lawyer, there's an essential need to engage the world," says Vice Dean Robert Ahdieh, a leading scholar on international financial regulation and trade.

Emory Law also provides a platform for those who want to delve more deeply into global legal issues. In the International Humanitarian Law Clinic, the only law clinic of its kind in the United States, students provide support for human rights organizations and help develop training materials related to the law of armed conflict. The student-run *Emory International Law Review* receives submissions from academics, professionals, and students around the world and brings leading thinkers to campus.

Academic centers—from the Project on War and Security in Law, Culture, and Society to the Global Health Law and Policy Project—focus on international problem-solving. Abdullahi Ahmed An-Na'im, director of the Center for International and Comparative Law and Charles Howard Candler Professor of Law, found a home at Emory Law after he was exiled from his native Sudan. He had

continued on page 55

Paying It Forward

FACUNDO BACARDI 96L

The principle of giving back to individuals and communities is important to my family. In 1960, our family's company of almost one hundred years was confiscated by a new communist Cuban government in the name of the Revolution. All of our personal assets, aside from what we could carry in a suitcase, were taken away as well. It is the same story that can be retold by hundreds of thousands of Cubans who sought a new life in the United States and elsewhere. Many of them were taken in by families of their newly adopted country who wanted to help in their own small way to provide relief to the less fortunate. These generous gestures enabled many Cubans to create new lives, provide for their families, and pursue success in their new countries. For us, kind acts of generosity led us to build back our businesses and eventually come to operate in 180 countries around the world. Most importantly, we are engaged on some level in most of those communities.

Reflecting on my three-year experience at Emory Law brings back happy memories, the most memorable being the opportunity to meet new people and make lifelong friendships with students and professors alike. Knowing my career would lie in the business world, I chose to attend Emory Law so that I could benefit from a rigorous legal education and develop a better understanding of the interaction between law and business. With this perspective in mind, I was free of the stresses law students typically endured as they sought internships and permanent positions, all the while wondering how they would meet their future school loan obligations. I had a strong sense of empathy for many students who were so deserving of just being able to focus on school and their careers in a positive way.

Also, my friendships with law professors allowed me to understand their efforts in educating future lawyers as their life's calling, and I saw their genuine interest in helping students realize professional goals. Over time, I realized I could play a small role by touching Emory's students and professors through my family's commitment to giving back to our many communities. My focus is to help minimize the financial implications a law school education may have on Emory's law students while celebrating the work of Emory professors through creating scholarships in their honor as an acknowledgment of a life well lived.

Giving back is a way my family continually expresses its thanks and gratitude for the care it received when it needed it most. For me, giving back to Emory is my way of supporting students who can make a difference in the future while giving thanks to Emory's professors who already made a difference.

Facundo Bacardi is a graduate of the Emory Law Class of 1996 and chairman of the board of Bacardi Limited.

The Path to Professionalism

Emory Law Builds Careers of Passion and Integrity

Communication is key when entering the law, Associate Dean A. James Elliott tells Emory Law students.

ancient and honorable profession of law. As students take their first steps in their legal education, they attend sessions that provide guideposts for integrity in their legal practice.

"We want our students to leave here not just knowing the model rules of conduct, but to understand the conduct of being a professional," says Associate Dean A. James Elliott, a former president of the State Bar of Georgia and cofounder of Emory Law's Professionalism Program, which received the Gambrell Professionalism Award from the American Bar Association in 1999.

In fall and spring sessions, practicing lawyers engage the students in conversations framed around hypothetical but realistic situations: What if you received a job offer based on your stellar first-year grades, but then your grades drop? What if you get an offer for a paying job just days before you are due to start an unpaid internship for a nonprofit legal aid organization? What if illness or a family emergency causes you to fall behind and you can't finish a work assignment by the deadline?

Full disclosure is the best policy, Elliott tells the student lawyers. "We want to embed in your minds that communication is key."

On the final day of orientation, after the ice-breaking and before the "paper chase" of the first semester, incoming Emory Law students pause for a serious moment—a swearing in.

They are still at least a year from earning the right to practice in a courtroom. (Georgia law allows second- and third-year law students to provide limited legal services under the supervision of a practicing attorney.)

But literally from day one, Emory Law sends a message about both the promise and responsibility of entering the

> **"We want our students to leave here not just knowing the model rules of conduct, but to understand the conduct of being a professional."**
>
> **—Associate Dean A. James Elliott**

continued from page 52

opposed the adoption of a severe form of Sharia law, advocacy that put him at risk of detention and execution for apostasy and treason.

He has never shied from controversy, whether he was opposing the war in Iraq or arguing
that Islam is properly practiced in a secular state that respects religious freedom (not the
"Islamic State"). His writings and research projects focus on Islamic law and human rights.
"I think of Emory as a very fresh place, a place willing to be open," An-Na'im says. "There's a
willingness to take risks and to open new avenues of thinking."

Emory also has attracted an unprecedented number of international students, who either
seek career opportunities in the United States or hope to bring their knowledge of US law
back to their home countries.

"We prepare students to be leaders in a globalized world and to bring a global focus to
their careers," says Dean Robert Schapiro.

*Abdullahi Ahmed An-Na'im,
Charles Howard Candler
Professor of Law, is a world-
renowned scholar of Islam
and human rights.*

Emory Law's emergence as a truly
global law school parallels the transformation of its hometown. In 1971,
Atlanta had only one international
flight (to Mexico City), but it had big
dreams. City boosters once again
ramped up a significant marketing campaign, calling Atlanta "the
world's next great city."

Just as the city was yearning
for greatness, Emory University
received a gift that would enable
it to chart a dramatic trajectory.
In 1979, former Coca-Cola president Robert Woodruff, along with
his brother George, liquidated the
Emily and Ernest Woodruff Fund
and transferred its assets—$105
million of Coca-Cola Company

Robert W. Woodruff Professor of Law Michael J. Perry specializes in constitutional law, human rights, and law and religion.

stock—to Emory University. It immediately boosted the university's endowment to the top tier among US schools and put Emory on the map as a leading university.

"Emory certainly grew across the board—in stature and fundamental strength," says Tom Morgan, Emory Law's dean from 1980 to 1985. "It wasn't the amount of the dollars [that made the difference]. It was the message the gift conveyed."

That infusion enabled Emory Law to attract top legal scholars for Robert W. Woodruff Professorships, the university's most esteemed academic appointment. Harold Berman, an expert in Soviet law, legal history, and law and religion at Harvard Law School, was the first to receive the honor when he came to Emory in 1985. For the next twenty-two years, Berman pioneered the study of comparative law, legal history, and law and religion at Emory Law. He founded the American Law Center in Moscow, a joint venture of Emory Law and the Law Academy of the Russian Ministry of Justice, as well as the Russian Studies Program at the Carter Center.

Today's Woodruff Professors push the boundaries of their respective fields. Martha Fineman moves beyond the traditional paradigms of gender, race, privilege, and disadvantage in her exploration of the theory of human vulnerability. John Witte stokes dialogue around the world about the fundamentals of faith, freedom, and the family. Michael Perry pursues constitutional studies through the lens of political morality and human rights theory.

They join other prominent legal scholars on the Emory Law faculty. "It's only fitting that those of us who occupy these [law faculty] positions are not just teaching students but serving society," Perry says. "You're dealing with issues that are front and center for society."

▼ ▼ ▼

In 1987, Atlanta attorney Billy Payne began the quixotic campaign that eventually brought the 1996 Olympic Games to the city. In its own realm, Emory Law had already begun to forge global connections.

Harold Berman recruited Thomas Buergenthal, a renowned human rights lawyer who later became a member of the International Court of Justice, to join the Emory Law faculty in 1985. Buergenthal, who also directed the Carter Center's program on human rights, prompted Emory Law to add a new master of comparative law degree as a gateway for international students.

Meanwhile, tumult in the world meant shifting alliances—and new opportunities. Tibor Varady, a law professor and justice minister in the former Yugoslavia, became a man without a country and found a new home at Emory Law, where he had been a visiting professor.

As the Cold War ended and the Soviet Union dissolved, Dean Howard "Woody" Hunter saw that Emory Law could take a greater role in the new global dynamic. He built on a partnership with Central European University in Budapest, where Varady also taught. Emory Law

Barbara Woodhouse, one of the world's experts on children's rights, is director of the Child Rights Project.

Harold Berman, the first Robert W. Woodruff Professor of Law, was a pioneer in the study of law and religion and one of the world's foremost scholars in Soviet and post-Soviet law.

David Bederman, who argued before the US Supreme Court four times, founded Emory Law's Supreme Court Advocacy Project.

students could spend a semester in Budapest and a semester in Atlanta for a master of laws (LLM) degree. That relationship continues today, and Emory Law JD students also can spend a semester abroad in Germany, Australia, Singapore, China, South Korea, Switzerland, or Ireland.

David Bederman joined the faculty in 1991, bringing a broad devotion to scholarship that encompassed admiralty law, legal history, and international law. Appointed as the K. H. Gyr Professor of Private International Law, he argued before the US Supreme Court four times and founded Emory Law's Supreme Court Advocacy Project.

When David Tkeshelashvili 06L, then an environment minister in the Republic of Georgia, received an LLM from Emory Law through an Edmund S. Muskie Scholarship, he initiated a lasting relationship between the Law School and his homeland. Today, international students are a mainstay of the Emory Law community.

Stefania Alessi 17L has a law degree from the University of Palermo in her home country of Italy and a master of laws from the University of Chicago. But that was not enough. From Chicago, she made her way to Emory Law for an accelerated juris doctor (AJD), a two-year program that enables foreign-trained lawyers to take the bar exam anywhere in the United States.

With fellow students from around the world—China, South Korea, India, Haiti, Ghana, and Venezuela, among other countries—Alessi blended into the traditional coursework, which includes legal writing. By the end of her first year at Emory, Alessi secured a summer position at a Chicago law firm that may become a permanent position. "I saw the reality of the legal world in the United States, and I never want to go back," she says.

Hooran Sun spent a gap year in his Shanghai law program learning about the US legal system. Instead of studying legal codes, he learned from cases. Instead of crafting arguments for judges, he learned how US lawyers approach a jury.

"To let a jury decide the outcome of a case is unpredictable—but the outcome could be [more] convincing to the common people," he says.

From Local to International—Emory Law School's Evolution

NAT GOZANSKY

When I came to Emory University School of Law in 1967 it was best described as a regional law school. There were no *U.S. News & World Report* rankings, though folks in the Southeast viewed Emory, Duke, and Vanderbilt as the big three at the time. Emory had a part-time evening program that was a reflection of its origins and, to some extent, its focus.

Dean Ben Johnson represented Emory in its 1962 lawsuit to strike down the state legislation that prevented us from enrolling students of color and focused on diversifying the student body. He also tapped federal funding to open two free legal aid offices for the poor, and in doing so provided Emory Law students a substantial clinical opportunity. The legal aid offices, along with a diversifying faculty, helped launch Emory Law down its long evolutionary road toward national prominence.

Following the dedication of Gambrell Hall in the early 1970s—Emory Law's new home—came rapid expansion of the student body and the faculty. L. Ray Patterson, formerly of the Vanderbilt law faculty, assumed the deanship from Johnson and began building relationships with elite undergraduate schools in the Northeast and Midwest. By the end of Patterson's tenure, the student body was majority nonsouthern.

When Tom Morgan assumed the deanship, in turn, he focused on curricular reform and enhancing faculty research.

He also recruited Tom Buergenthal, an internationally recognized human rights scholar and a Holocaust survivor, to move the Law School into international venues. Buergenthal helped introduce a new master of comparative law (MCL) degree program designed exclusively for foreign-trained lawyers who sought legal study in the United States. While the MCL program was successful—it brought a dozen or so young scholars to the Law School each year—it fell into quiescence after Buergenthal returned to Washington, DC, to teach. (It was recently reinstated, in an exciting partnership with Shanghai Jiao Tong University's KoGuan Law School.)

The path to national—and increasingly global—prominence gained further traction as Emory Law focused on recruiting faculty with international backgrounds. Under Dean David Epstein, the Law School attracted international law faculty, including Peter Hay, Tibor Varady, and Johan van der Vyver. Later, Dean Howard Hunter brought Abdullahi An-Na'im and others on board, to establish further international ties.

Students were encouraged to study abroad, including through student exchange programs with schools in Europe, Asia, and Australia. Later, Emory Law hired staff to aggressively attract foreign lawyers to the master of laws (LLM) and other graduate programs. And as a result, today there are about two hundred international students pursuing graduate degrees at the Law School each year. The school also hosts foreign scholars on research leave from their home schools.

With its programs, faculty, and students, Emory Law has become a truly global law school.

Professor Emeritus Nat Gozansky retired from Emory Law in 2012 after forty-five years of service.

Fulfilling the Dream

Career Guidance Starts on Day One—
and Lasts a Lifetime

Emory Law students begin envisioning their future careers even before they arrive on campus. Some have a clear direction. Others feel unsure about their options. But they are not alone in their quest. Turning their aspirations into reality is an enduring partnership, bolstered by an extensive alumni network and support from the Center for Professional Development and Career Strategy.

The guidance starts early. In September, 1Ls attend the Bass Career Summit, where they learn some basics about how to match their skills and interests with different types of legal practice.

A few weeks later, the Kagan-Horowitz Practice Society Premiere introduces 1Ls to the Law School's student practice societies and gives them their first taste of networking. By joining a practice society, they gain a tangible and valuable link between their academic study and the legal profession.

The Career Center's twelve career advisers work one-on-one with students, helping them select courses that match their professional interests. Students gain career skills from interactive workshops and panel discussions, lessons in business etiquette and advice on how to shape their resumes, and attending mock interviews and networking receptions.

Emory Law gives students a further edge by offering the Bridge to Practice Fellowship. With the fellowship, a modest monthly stipend supports work at a public interest organization or government agency. New graduates can prove themselves and gain a foothold into their dream job.

Law firms once provided extensive additional training to new associates, but with cutbacks, they now often favor lawyers who have at least one or two years of experience. The Emory Law Hiring Initiative responded to that trend by offering funding for initial training, taking the burden off of law firms. "We have more than twenty graduates who are now in permanent positions because the firms decided to hire them due to this initiative," says Lydia Russo, assistant dean for the Center for Professional Development and Career Strategy.

More than 95 percent of Emory Law graduates report that they are employed within months of graduation, almost all of them in positions that require bar admission. But the career guidance does not end there. The Career Center continues to connect them with alumni and helps them secure a second position—or other future job.

"We are here for you," Russo tells graduates. "The whole reason our office exists is to help these students become the lawyers they want to be."

Students receive personalized career guidance at Emory Law, with opportunities to hone their interview skills and network with practitioners.

Law professors craft hypotheticals to teach students how to approach legal problems. Today, these hypotheticals reflect complexities that would have been unthinkable just a decade ago. In its scholarship and teaching, Emory Law also crosses boundaries, embracing innovation and creativity, and developing new programs to meet emerging needs.

The study of law is relevant even to a broad range of students who have no intention of pursuing a legal career. Instead, they seek career advantage from having a strong understanding of the legal issues they will encounter in a different profession. In 2011, Emory Law began offering a juris master for professionals and students in other fields. After taking several core courses, the JM students may select a concentration, such as employment law, health law, or compliance/business.

In the business arena, the new millennium spawned a startup culture that has redefined the realm of intellectual property. Through a unique partnership with the Georgia Institute of Technology, Emory Law students join MBA and engineering doctoral students on teams charged with developing promising ideas into new companies. In Technological Innovation: Generating Economic Results (TI:GER), law students take foundational courses, such as patent law and Fundamentals of Innovation, then work on the entrepreneurial teams.

Recent student projects have included a medical device to improve the outcome of spinal surgery and a new material that reduces heat in electronic devices. The legal dimension is an essential part of technology commercialization, says Marie Thursby, an entrepreneurship

Professor Jennifer Mathews works with a Juris master (JM) student. Many JM students are working professionals who select concentrations specific to their interests, such as employment or health law.

Professor Nicole Morris directs the TI:GER program, a unique partnership with the Georgia Institute of Technology on technology commercialization.

professor at Georgia Tech and founding director of TI:GER. And the program ensures that students understand it.

Emory's TI:GER students provide advice about the corporate structure of the startups and the protection of intellectual property, and they gain insight from being on an entrepreneurial team. "Law students learn about business, business students learn about legal principles, and they work together in a team," says Nicole N. Morris, director of TI:GER and professor of practice, who specializes in intellectual property and patent law.

The TI:GER program's success inspired a similar connection with social entrepreneurs. Emory Law students can now join Catalyzing Social Impacts in the Goizueta Business School and work alongside MBA students, offering advice to clients (both for-profit and nonprofit) striving to have a positive social impact.

Even if the students go on to work for a large law firm, they have learned essential skills and gained a new perspective.

Bryan Stewart 12L worked with Spheringenics, a startup seeking to develop a new technology to improve cell-based medical therapies. He is now an associate with the technology and intellectual property group at Morris, Manning & Martin in Atlanta.

"Being able to understand some of the issues startups face really helps me with my practice," Stewart says. "It helped me understand how my clients view the world and what issues they are most interested in."

♥ ♥ ♥

Every entrepreneur fears the theft of a valuable idea. In a stealthy cyberworld, secrets are compromised and intellectual property is stolen every day, Steven Grimberg 98L, an Emory Law adjunct professor, told the audience at a recent Thrower Symposium, an annual gathering that recognizes renowned tax lawyer Randolph Thrower.

"This is one of the greatest threats to our economy today—modern-day espionage of nation-states stealing trade secrets," said Grimberg, who is deputy chief of economic crimes at the US Attorney's Office for the Northern District of Georgia.

How can you impose a rule of law on the lawless? We live in a dangerous world of terror cells and suicide bombers, of rogue states with nuclear weapons, of conflicts that seem to have no end. What is the role of law in the midst of bloody chaos?

From Gambrell Hall to World Headlines

Aloke Chakravarty 97L

Patriots' Day 2013. Within minutes, it was clear the Boston Marathon was under attack. I sprinted across town from my office to the FBI. Hundreds of police and agents swarmed in and out as we set up a command post. They rushed to the victims and began the hunt for the culprits. As an assistant US Attorney, I was the nation's lawyer on the front line during the crisis that followed. It was my job to uphold the legal rigor of the investigation, to find creative solutions to roadblocks, to be temperate where necessary, and to preserve a prosecution if there would be one. It was an awesome responsibility.

My ability to make that impact began with values that were cultivated at Emory Law. In Gambrell Hall I learned that how you practice the law is as important as how well you practice. The relationships that I had built in my years as a prosecutor were forged on the strength of collaboration, integrity, and judgment. These Emory values built a trust with the rest of the team that carried me in the days after the bombings through the end of the trial.

This was not a surprise, because I had chosen Emory based on its reputation as a champion of human dignity; whether at home or abroad, the university has helped shape lives for the better. So when I graduated, I very much wanted to be part of something greater than myself. I chose the path of public service. After September 11, 2001, I steered toward the challenge of national security while respecting civil rights. At the time, few who looked like me were being consulted, let alone making the tough choices about where those lines should be drawn on a day-to-day basis. I found our national security efforts were more effective when they conspicuously adhered to the rule of law.

Emory Law validated this path by allowing me to discover and play to my strengths. Through the Trial Techniques program and a class called Persuasion and Drama, I embraced trial advocacy—a world I could excel in and enjoy. It empowered me to trust in myself and my choice of craft. It gave me the hope that someday I could stand up for an injured client, in a case that might be important to more than just the parties.

I relied on all of this, and more, during the trial that would follow—one watched around the world and a test of American justice in a new era of global threats. At the trial, through agonizing testimony, victims and responders personified the dignity of humanity and personal excellence, values I had hoped to vindicate when I chose to go to law school. The decisions we made were colored by this responsibility of achieving justice while also showing the fairness and strength of our system. Using the power of narrative and multimedia technology, we showed the story, bringing the type of moral persuasion that comes with demonstrating a historical truth. When I finished the closing argument, the world may not have recognized Emory Law's influence in the case, but for me, its values had shaped not just what to present, but how to do so. In crisis situations, people rely on their training and their values. The Law School served me well on both fronts.

Aloke Chakravarty is a graduate of the Emory Law Class of 1997. He is assistant US Attorney for the US Attorney's Office for the District of Massachusetts. In May 2015, he won a death penalty verdict against Dzhokhar Tsarnaev, the surviving brother responsible for the Boston Marathon bombing.

Professor Laurie Blank directs the International Humanitarian Law Clinic, the only one of its kind in the United States.

Emory Law probes these and other difficult questions. In the International Humanitarian Law Clinic, Professor Laurie Blank guides her students through the law of armed conflict, which addresses issues such as the humane treatment of detainees and the protection of civilians during wartime. "The idea of mitigating suffering in war is to preserve human dignity and help enable a sustainable peace afterward," says Blank.

Through their work with the International Humanitarian Law Clinic, Emory Law students have had a lasting influence. They have assisted attorneys who represent detainees at the Guantanamo Bay Detention Center in Cuba. They worked with the Special Tribunal for Lebanon, formed by the United Nations to investigate the 2005 assassination of the prime minister and the deaths of twenty-two other people. They helped to incorporate the law of war and international law into the curriculum at the Marine Corps University in Quantico, Virginia. Graduates of the clinic now work at the US Department of State, the International Criminal Court, and the Judge Advocate General's Corps of all four branches of the US military.

> **"Law has become recognized around the world as an important force. And the kind of legal education that we offer in the United States—and specifically at Emory—is simply not attainable any other place in the world."**
>
> **—Dean Robert Schapiro**

This international involvement reveals just how relevant legal education is in a tumultuous world. "There's a growing recognition of the power of law around the world. That's why people from emerging economies come to Emory to study law," says Dean Robert Schapiro.

In its earliest days, Emory Law had the goal of improving the caliber of the legal profession in Georgia and the South. Today, Emory Law seeks a global impact, by fostering conversation and scholarship, contributing pro bono work, welcoming diverse students and faculty, adhering to high standards, and—most importantly—educating a new generation of lawyers with a broad perspective.

"Law has become recognized around the world as an important force," says Schapiro. "And the kind of legal education that we offer in the United States—and specifically at Emory—is simply not attainable any other place in the world." ♦

INDEX